"Elizabeth Evans has written a book of daily devotions that delves into the heart and life issues of those who bear the pain of unfulfilled expectations. While she focuses each amazing chapter on the issue of infertility, the lessons she learned from God and His Word are applicable to virtually anyone. Saturated in prayerful thought and scriptural truth, this message of hope came from her heart and will reach yours as it did mine. Take time to read the words and feel the strength of life woven into each daily focus. Your investment of time will be well rewarded. Beth's life   help you find that flicker of light that we

—*Edwin Jenkins, in*
Morgan B

"With her personal stories, heartfelt convictions, and beautiful conversational style, Elizabeth Evans, in her new daily devotional book, *30 Days of Hope for Comfort in Infertility*, walks tenderly alongside women who yearn to become mothers, yet struggle with the pain of infertility. Offering hope and keen insight into a deeper relationship with Christ, Evans ministers to women with Scripture, encouragement, biblical understanding, and prayer. I highly recommend Evans's new book, as well as her previous book, *30 Days of Hope for Strength in Chronic Illness.*"

—*Denise George, author of 30 books, speaker, and writing-to-publish teacher with The Book Writing Boot Camp*

"Anyone who knew Elizabeth recognized the deep compassion she held toward others who suffered. Whatever difficult situation life brought her, her aim was to help others who might experience a similar path. *30 Days of Hope for Comfort in Infertility* embodies Beth's desire to make the road easier for others experiencing the infertility she faced. She uses Scripture, story, and the presence of God to bring her readers comfort with every page. I encourage any woman facing infertility or any friend walking alongside to take this 30-day journey of hope with Beth."

—*Andrea Mullins, retired publisher, New Hope Publishers*

"Although the reasons for being barren are different for each of us, we all have a deep pain in the bottom of our hearts that seems to take full control at times. If you are struggling with the issues of infertility or trying to understand why God's plan for you does not include motherhood, then please read this book. If you love someone going through either of these issues, please give this book to them."

—*Shannon Williams, cousin of Elizabeth Evans*

30 DAYS OF HOPE

FOR COMFORT IN INFERTILITY

ELIZABETH EVANS

NEW HOPE®
PUBLISHERS
Gospel-Centered. Missions-Driven.

BIRMINGHAM, ALABAMA

New Hope® Publishers
PO Box 12065
Birmingham, AL 35202-2065
NewHopePublishers.com
New Hope Publishers is a division of WMU®.

Library of Congress Cataloging-in-Publication Data

Names: Evans, G. Elizabeth, 1966- author.
Title: 30 days of hope for comfort in infertility / Elizabeth Evans.
Other titles: Thirty days of hope for comfort in infertility
Description: Birmingham, AL : New Hope Publishers, 2016.
Identifiers: LCCN 2016020053 (print) | LCCN 2016026685 (ebook) |
    ISBN 9781596694644 (sc) | ISBN 9781596699427 (e-book)
Subjects: LCSH: Christian women--Prayers and devotions. |
    Infertility--Religious aspects--Christianity. | Consolation.
Classification: LCC BV4527 .E895 2016 (print) | LCC BV4527 (ebook) |
    DDC 242/.4--dc23
LC record available at Library of Congress LCCN Permalink for 2016020053

ISBN-10: 1-59669-464-5
ISBN-13: 978-1-59669-464-4

N164104 • 0916 • 1M1

THIS BOOK IS DEDICATED TO MY MOTHER,

GRACE BALLARD,

FROM WHOM ALL THE GREAT LESSONS OF LIFE AND MOTHERING
CAME. MY MOTHER IS AN AMAZING GODLY WOMAN OF STRENGTH
BEYOND DESCRIPTION. HER LOVE, PATIENCE, AND COMPASSION
HAVE ALWAYS BEEN THERE TO GUIDE AND COMFORT ME.
HER LOVE FOR HER LORD, HER HUSBAND, AND HER CHILDREN
HAS BEEN MY SUSTAINING STRENGTH.

I LOVE YOU, MOTHER.
YOU REALLY ARE MY HERO!

TABLE OF CONTENTS

ACKNOWLEDGMENTS 11

INTRODUCTION 13

DAY 1: Born to Be Mommies 17

DAY 2: Earnest Expectation 21

DAY 3: The Heart of a Mother 25

DAY 4: Tunnel Vision 29

DAY 5: Dreaming of Motherhood 33

DAY 6: Desperately Longing 37

DAY 7: Shattered Dreams 41

DAY 8: Why? Why? Why? 45

DAY 9: Disillusioned 49

DAY 10: Discouraged 53

DAY 11: Disappointed 57

DAY 12: Devastated 61

DAY 13: Disconnected 65

DAY 14: Depressed 69

SHANNON'S STORY 73

DAY 15: Emotionally Ambushed 75

DAY 16: Hurt 79

DAY 17: Anger 83

DAY 18: Guilt 87

DAY 19: Betrayal 91

DAY 20: Grief 95

DAY 21: Despair 99

MY STORY 102

DAY 22: A Happy Woman 105

DAY 23: Grace to Sustain 109

DAY 24: God's Plan Is Perfect 113

DAY 25: The Greater Picture 117

DAY 26: Blessings in Disguise 121

DAY 27: Gifts of Grace 125

DAY 28: Be Settled 129

DAY 29: Contentment in Christ 133

DAY 30: Beauty out of Barrenness 137

ACKNOWLEDGEMENTS

I WANT to say a very special thanks to my "sissy" for allowing me to share a portion of her story through this work. She and I traveled two unique journeys through barrenness. God brought us to different places and, where my pain has been soothed, hers—as of yet—has not. I pray that she also will gain strength and peace from this book, which she helped inspire. Thank you, Sissy. I love you dearly!

I also want to express my gratitude to my Lord and Savior Jesus Christ for the soothing salve of the Holy Spirit, through whom only I have found peace and contentment in barrenness. May He alone be glorified by what has been written on these pages.

INTRODUCTION

B ARRENNESS: it's a biblical word, but a harsh-sounding one nevertheless. It's a word that could be used of a desert or a landscape devoid of growth—or the backside of the moon. Unfortunately, the word is most often associated with women who have not given birth to a child. Barrenness describes too well the dashed hopes and lack of fulfillment that often plague women who struggle with it. Maybe that is why today we usually use the more clinical term: *infertility*.

This book, *30 Days of Hope for Comfort in Infertility*, deals with the extremely sensitive issues and raw emotions that women encounter when they are in the midst of desperately desiring to conceive. It also examines the discouragement of those who have been devastated by the realization that they are not able to conceive.

I will share with you the emotions and inner struggles I encountered as I traveled through my journey of—yes, I will use the word—barrenness. Longing, hurt, anger, confusion, disillusionment, and feelings of failure are all part of the stigma we attach to ourselves (and believe others attach to us) when we cannot conceive. My prayer is that as you read about my experience, you will see into my heart, feel my struggles, and find encouragement in knowing you are not alone. I desperately want to help bring understanding that no matter how negative your thoughts and feelings may be, they are normal. Despite the validity of your feelings, I assure you that no matter where you are physically, emotionally, or spiritually in this journey, there is hope, healing, inner peace, and contentment available through Christ.

I will candidly address the issues I found that infertility brings with it, such as:

- Depression
- Feelings of inadequacy
- Questions of why
- Disillusionment about your role as a wife
- Painful envy when those around you experience the joy of conception
- Desperate longing for a love not yet known

My hope is that you will be encouraged, comforted, and assured—despite the fact of barrenness—hope is found in and through Christ and only through Christ. Allowing Him to bring you full circle in your personal journey can create beauty out of barrenness.

DAY 1

BORN TO BE MOMMIES

As for you, be fruitful and increase in number;
multiply on the earth and increase upon it.

—Genesis 9:7 NIV

A s LITTLE girls, it is engrained in most of us early that one day we will be mommies. We pretend to feed our baby dolls in toy high chairs. We dress them and take them for walks in miniature strollers. We even pretend to change diapers (minus any of the sights and smells of reality). With more maturity we may be given some responsibility for younger siblings. Watching our own mothers, we learn how to mother. And we naturally assume that when we grow up we will have babies of our own.

Our natural maternal instincts were placed in us by God before the foundation of the world. However, what happens to our spirit, soul, and psyche when motherhood does not come as naturally as we had hoped or we are given a devastating diagnosis of the impossibility of bearing children?

I have been down this unwanted and uncharted road myself. Everyone's journey is unique in its struggles, emotions, and eventual outcomes. However, as God's precious creation, we are loved beyond our ability to understand, and our feelings of devastation, anger, and inadequacy are understood more than we can comprehend.

Wherever you are on your journey, whether you are having difficulty conceiving, in the midst of fertility treatments, or maybe living with the reality of being unable to have your own children, God has created you for a purpose. We are taught from childhood that our purpose is to be mommies, and we never consider that God may have a different plan for our lives. It is not that He desires for us to be childless, He just may have another plan on how He will satisfy that longing He placed in us to mother.

Yield your journey to motherhood to God. Allow Him to soothe your aching heart. He not only sees your tears but he collects them. As Psalm 56:8 (NKJV) says, "You number my wanderings; Put my tears into Your bottle; Are they not in Your book?"

He knows your concerns, and He is attentive to those concerns. The psalmist tells us, "Take delight in the Lord, and he will give you the desires of your heart" (Psalm 37:4 NIV). This only happens when we are willing to align our desires with His plans and desires for our life.

Dear Lord,
I know You have placed the instincts
and desires to mother in my heart.
My prayer is that I would yield myself
to Your plan for my life, willingly
and completely. I pray that You will
soothe my aching heart and place all
my tears in Your bottle. Thank You
for the plan You have for my life, and
I look forward to how those plans will
be fulfilled. Amen.

DAY 2

EARNEST EXPECTATION

*So be strong and courageous, all you who put your
hope in the Lord!*

—Psalm 31:24

Hope: "earnest expectation," as defined
by *Strong's Exhaustive Concordance.*

A T AGE 23, I found myself married and planning a family of my own. My husband had sole custody of his two boys, ages two and three. So when we married, I became an instant mommy. However, we both desired to have a child together. Even though I had been discouraged by my doctors and knew that the statistics at that time showed that chances were not good for women with cystic fibrosis to get pregnant, endure pregnancy, or live to their full potential or life expectancy if they give birth, I had hope—earnest expectation—and was determined.

Month after month after month, we were disappointed. I understood the statistics weren't encouraging, but I hoped each month that I would learn that I was expecting. However, each month I was faced with disappointment. All the time I relished being a mommy to two of the most beautiful little boys. To them I was Mommy. And, on a day-to-day basis, I did all of the things a mommy does with those two precious boys. Yet, I still longed to become pregnant, to feel a precious life growing inside of me.

Oh, what I was missing right in my own home and heart! I realize now that I never really embraced and praised God at that time for the opportunity to be a mommy—the opportunity He had already given me. I longed for what I did not have yet. What I wanted. What I thought I needed. What I even assumed was God's plan.

Sometimes we just run down our own pathway as fast as we can, following our own agenda, missing all the beauty surrounding us—unless it is exactly what we hope for, what we earnestly expect. We never see the unexpected beauty.

As a song title says, "Turn Your Eyes upon Jesus." We need to open not only our eyes but also our hearts to what God has for us. We must place our hope and earnest expectation in Him and Him alone. Our hope is not in plans for conception, doctors, or fertility treatments. Our hope is not in prayers or pleadings that our life's journey will be what we want. Our hope is in Him for whom nothing is impossible.

But now, Lord, what do I look for? My hope is in you.

—Psalm 39:7 NIV

Dear Lord,

I place all my hope in You today: the hope of conception, the hope of motherhood, the hope of what is in store for my life, my marriage, and my family. My hope is in You, Lord. I pray for forgiveness when I seek my own agenda instead of Yours. I ask that You would lovingly remind me that Your ways are higher than mine, and Your love for me is much more than I can comprehend. I know You desire only to love me and that Your plan is always to bring the best for my life. Amen.

DAY 3

THE HEART OF A MOTHER

Once after a sacrificial meal at Shiloh, Hannah got up and went to pray. Eli the priest was sitting at his customary place beside the entrance of the Tabernacle. Hannah was in deep anguish, crying bitterly as she prayed to the LORD. And she made this vow: "O LORD of Heaven's Armies, if you will look upon my sorrow and answer my prayer and give me a son, then I will give him back to you. He will be yours for his entire lifetime, and as a sign that he has been dedicated to the LORD, his hair will never be cut." . . . and in due time she gave birth to a son. She named him Samuel, for she said, "I asked the LORD for him."

—1 SAMUEL 1:9–11, 20

HANNAH is a classic example of barrenness in the Bible and the one every woman who struggles with infertility hopes will be her story. Hannah asked for a child. She cried out to God in her anguish, and He answered her prayer and gave her a child. She dedicated little Samuel totally to the Lord's service and took him, at a very young age, to live at the Tabernacle with a very old priest. Not an easy thing for a relatively new mother to do. But then God rewarded her faithfulness by giving her more children.

I am encouraged when I read about Hannah because I see in her the same emotions I have had. She wants children desperately. She cries bitterly out to God "in her anguish," yet God doesn't condemn her or reprimand her. It seems that the devastation connected with infertility can open an unfamiliar, even argumentative dialogue between us and the Lord. And I ask:

Why do I have reproductive organs if they don't work?
Why did You place this longing for motherhood in me if it's physically impossible?
Why don't you want me to be a mother?

Having faith does not mean that you will not have questions. It means you have you have a place to take them. God heard Hannah's cries, and He hears yours. You may not have the outcome that Hannah did, yet God is the same God. You may long to know exactly how or when God will answer your anguished prayers. Yet "we walk by faith, not by sight" 2 Corinthians 5:7 (NKJV). Continue to cry out to the Lord, knowing He hears you and has a special plan to fulfill the mother's heart He placed within you.

Dear Lord,
Just like Hannah, my heart cries out but words fail me. You know the yearnings within me. You know the questions within me. I trust in due time that I will see Your plan for this mother's heart come to fruition. Amen.

.

TUNNEL VISION

The L<small>ORD</small> says, "I will guide you along the best pathway
for your life. I will advise you and watch over you.
Do not be like a senseless horse or mule that needs a bit
and bridle to keep it under control."

—P<small>SALM</small> 32:8–9

J ust like most girls, I dreamed of having a baby. Being a mommy. Holding a tiny life in my arms and seeing myself and my husband reflected there. I never doubted my dreams would come true. I always saw myself this way. My plans were to marry, have babies, and live happily ever after. But . . . what was God's plan? I had not vacated my own ideas long enough to give that any consideration.

What if He had a different plan for my life? But then again, why would He? Had He not placed within me the desire for children? Why would He give me such longing for a love I couldn't know? I must be able to eventually bring forth children. I just assumed that. I never considered a different plan for my life. A better plan for my life. A bigger picture.

I had tunnel vision. I wanted to get pregnant and feel the miracle of that life growing inside me. I wanted to feel "whole" as a woman. I wanted to be a mommy just like all my friends and family.

You may find yourself feeling the same way, with tunnel vision. You constantly think about and plan for the day you will be pregnant. You imagine yourself in maternity clothes. You browse through the baby section and imagine all you will one day buy. You may even pick out designs you will use in your nursery.

Yet, the deeper you get into disappointment, month after month, your tunnel vision narrows. You do not allow yourself to think about the negative. You assume God's plan for your life rather than asking Him. You do not want to— nor can you—see the bigger picture. Even when your plans are broadsided by reality, you hold tight to your own plans, dreams, and hopes for the day you are pregnant.

Allow God to remove the blinders and lead you down the path He has for your life. He loves you more than you are capable of comprehending, and He has a plan that is perfect for you. Abandon the tunnel vision, allow Him to open your eyes!

Dear God,
You know my heart. You know the plans I have for my life. I trust You, Lord, and I trust Your plan for my life. Guide me down the path You have for me. I want to abandon my tunnel vision and allow You to open the eyes of my spirit. I want all You have designed for me. Lord, help me accept Your plan for my life. I love You, Lord. I give You praise now, even when I cannot see the outcome of my prayers or Your plans. Amen.

DAY 5

DREAMING OF MOTHERHOOD

The LORD is close to the brokenhearted;
he rescues those whose spirits are crushed.

—PSALM 34:18

EVERYONE in your circle—friends, co-workers, family, and church social group—is beginning their families. Not a week goes by that you do not hear of someone close to you sharing the joy, announcing, "We're having a baby!" While you smile on the outside, on the inside your heart begins to break, tears fall in your spirit, and you ask your question once again, "When will that be me?"

You purchased a gift for a baby shower while fighting through the tears. Yet, when the date arrived to attend, you manufactured a viable reason not to attend. You feel so ugly inside because you love your friends and family and you want their happiness, but your hurt is overwhelming, drowning out the joy you should feel for others. The conflict of emotions and your own confusion is blinding you to any needs but your own.

Others do not know your feelings, your struggles to conceive. They don't know how many times you thought it would be your turn to make that joyful announcement only to be disappointed once again. The excited expectation you have each month followed only by letdown. The dreams of turning that extra room into a nursery enveloped in pastels. The tears you have cried. The questions you have asked. The desire to know such joy. The sorrow that grows inside you.

God knows your hurt, your longing, and your fears. He understands your feelings. Allow yourself to be transparent with Him, leaning on Him for the strength to continue to hope. Only He knows the plan for your life. Only His timing is perfect. He captures those tears you shed when someone else's joy reignites your pain. He longs to hold you close as you utter your petitions to Him through sobs. His grace is what enables you to continue to dream.

Dear Lord,

Only You know my heart, and You alone understand the conflict of emotions I feel. Only You can soothe my pain and help to sort out all my feelings. Please Lord, be with me. Help me to be joyful for others even though my heart is breaking. Remind me to lean on You. Draw me close. I give you praise for hearing and answering my prayers! Amen.

DAY 6

DESPERATELY LONGING

All my longings lie open before you, Lord;
my sighing is not hidden from you.
My heart pounds, my strength fails me;
even the light has gone from my eyes.

—Psalm 38:9–10 NIV

I LOVE the movie *Steel Magnolias*. In the movie, one of the main characters has a severe form of diabetes. Her relationship with her mother reminds me of my relationship with my mother as a teen and young adult. They struggle to be the independent women they both know they are deep inside, yet they somehow hold onto that nurturing mother-child relationship that they had always known and needed.

The daughter gets married and, against her doctor's advice, gets pregnant. When the daughter tells her mother the news of her pregnancy, the mom is openly hurt and even angry. The daughter is confused and taken back by the reaction that she gets. While the daughter is elated over her news, the mother, due to the doctor's warning, is worried and disheartened by the choice her daughter has made. An argument ensues. The two battle back and forth with hurtful comments rooted in love, confusion, and even pain.

The mother tries with everything in her power to hold onto her child. The daughter clings for dear life to the hopeful expectancy of holding her own child. As the mother finally breaks under her state of confusion, the daughter says to her, "I would rather have 30 minutes of wonderful than a lifetime of nothing special." At that moment, no matter how selfish the desire, the mother understands her child's heart. She too had known such a longing.

As a young woman, I had the same longing. Despite all warnings, and the statistics of what might happen to my body due to cystic fibrosis, I was willing to risk it all. I was willing to abandon everything for that one thing that seemed unattainable.

Through God's graciousness and her unconditional love, my mother never said a word. Because of her mother's heart, she knew my heart. She knew that longing. Her knowledge created a longing of her own. She longed for me to have the desire of my heart, even if that could ultimately cause the brokenness of her own.

The longing in your heart was placed there by a loving Heavenly Father who wants to fulfill it. However, His ways are not our ways, nor are His thoughts or His plans like ours (Isaiah 55:8–9). Take your longing to Him. He desires for your life to be wonderful. You may feel as though time is against you. But God is for you, and He will fulfill your longing in a way that will bring honor and glory to Him.

Dear Heavenly Father,
I feel at times that my longings will
never be fulfilled. At times they are
so overwhelming I feel as though I
will be crushed. Lord, I seek peace
and joy from You alone as I walk
this pathway. In the precious name of
Jesus, I pray. Amen.

DAY 7

SHATTERED DREAMS

To all who mourn in Israel, he will give a crown of beauty for ashes, a joyous blessing instead of mourning, festive praise instead of despair. In their righteousness, they will be like great oaks that the LORD has planted for his own glory.

—ISAIAH 61:3

ONE particular month, I was sure I was pregnant. I began to experience some of the symptoms of pregnancy. (I purchased a book about pregnancy, and I knew the symptoms by heart.) At the time, I had limited insurance. Pregnancy tests were fairly new and still quite expensive. Early one Saturday, I went to a local clinic that offered free testing.

At the clinic my urine test was negative, but the nurse was sure by my description that I was expecting. She thought it might still be too early to show up in the urine and decided to do a blood test to confirm a positive or negative decision. I was informed that the blood test results would take a few days, but they assured me they would call as soon as they got the results.

For the next several days, I anxiously awaited the news and raced to the phone every time it rang. I will never forget the day that the clinic called to tell me the results. When I answered, the person on the other end asked for me by name. I knew this was the call I had been waiting for, and I began to shake. Butterflies were soaring in my stomach. As she began, "I regret to inform you," my heart broke. I knew what the rest of the sentence was, "the test was negative. I am sorry but you are not pregnant at this time."

"Not this time? Not last time or any time," I said to myself. I hung up the phone and began to sob. I cried out to God, "Why not?" I wanted it so badly, more than I had ever wanted anything in my life. I wanted to have a baby. I wanted to feel that joy that new mothers felt when they held their baby for the first time. I wanted to know what it was like to look into the smiling face of your own child. Later that same day, I was hit even harder with the reality of my infertility. I can still see myself sitting on the end of my bed, bending over my dresser drawer, all the while crying out loud as my hurt overwhelmed me.

You may know and understand this story very well. You know the excitement, the hope, and then the devastating letdown. The breaking of your heart as you once again have your dreams shattered with a negative test or procedure result. Maybe you have even experienced a miscarriage. Whatever you are experiencing or have experienced, give it to God. Cry out to Him. He alone can truly know your heart, your hurt. He alone can soothe it. He wants you whole, not broken. Run to Him with your shattered pieces; He will create a beautiful mosaic to honor Him.

Dear Lord,
I come to You with my brokenness. I
cannot go on hurting this way. Lord,
hear my cry from the depths of my
innermost being and bring peace.
Thank You for hearing and answering
my prayer. Amen.

DAY 8

WHY? WHY? WHY?

Ask me and I will tell you remarkable secrets you do not know about things to come.

—JEREMIAH 33:3

W HY *am I not pregnant yet? Why can't I get pregnant? Why didn't the fertility drugs work? Why didn't the in vitro fertilization procedure yield positive results? Why do I continue to miscarry? Why is she pregnant, when I have been trying so much longer? Why is teen pregnancy so rampant when they cannot take care of their babies and I can? Why can women who abuse their bodies with drugs and alcohol get pregnant and I can't? Why are they having another baby when they don't have custody of the others they have conceived? Why? Why? Why?*

Those questions may seem harsh when they are printed on a page, yet they are all questions we have asked of God. I asked them over and over. I remember an instance where the evening news told of a teacher who had molested a student and gotten pregnant. She had gone to jail. However, while serving her prison term, she became pregnant—for the second time—with the same teen. I went into my small walk-in closet, closed the door, and screamed at God. Why?! Why does someone like her keep having babies, and here I am begging for a baby and I am still barren? That's not fair! Why, God? Why? I fell to the floor sobbing uncontrollably.

I recall a conversation that I had with my sister-in-law during her pregnancy. She called one afternoon to complain about the stress of pregnancy on her body and how tired she was. After a few minutes of listening to her complaints, as politely as possible at the time, I suggested that she might want to complain to someone else because I would give anything to be in her uncomfortable position. Sobbing, I hung up the phone and, for a moment, I wanted to curse God. I thought about how Job's wife encouraged him to curse God and die when he was suffering from monumental loss. But Job wouldn't curse God (Job 2:9–10). Instead of cursing, once again I asked God the question, "Why not me?"

God knows your heart and thoughts, whether spoken aloud or kept within. He also understands those feelings and questions. He placed that longing in your heart, but only He knows when and how it will be fulfilled. The question for you to answer is, do you trust God? Do you believe that He only wants the best for your life? Do you trust Him to heal your hurt, give you peace, and settle you, even in barrenness?

Dear Lord,
I have so many questions. You know
them all, and I am thankful You
understand my questions and pain.
I pray that as I question You, that I
would be aware of Your questions for
me. I do trust You and Your plan for
my life. I trust You will heal my hurt,
give me peace, and settle me, even in
my barrenness. Amen.

DISILLUSIONED

Hope deferred makes the heart sick,
but a dream fulfilled is a tree of life.

—Proverbs 13:12

Disillusioned: having lost faith or trust in something:
disappointed that something is not as you expected,
according to *Merriam-Webster's Dictionary*.

From birth, females are destined by social design to be "mommies." We are given baby dolls, strollers, toy baby furniture, miniature kitchens, etc. Everything a girl could want. The thought of not being a mommy is never considered by most of us. Then, when we grow up, get married, and don't have children—or don't do so in the expected time period—people begin to ask, "Are you planning to have children?" Or worse, "Why don't y'all have children yet?" In all fairness, unless the inquirers have experienced barrenness themselves or experienced it with a family member, they never think how those questions can be intrusive and extremely hurtful.

Even now, I cringe inside when I hear those questions being asked of a young woman or young couple. They can be asked in total innocence and genuineness. However, that does not lessen the pain inflicted on those who are in the midst of struggles to conceive. Least of all on those living with the reality of barrenness.

I want to offer encouragement to you, as someone who has taken this journey myself. Whatever you may have lost faith in, whatever your disappointment that things have not happened as you expected, God has not forgotten you. His timing is perfect. The time may come when you conceive, adopt, foster, or even marry into motherhood. I know how impatient you are. I know that not only are you asking *if* but *when*. You want to experience what all your friends are experiencing, but you cannot presume to know the plans of God. However, you can know His love, mercy, and grace. Give your disillusionment to God. He will sustain you and see you through. He will never leave you nor forsake you (Hebrews 13:5).

Dear Lord,
I have always expected to be a mommy.
I place my hope and trust in You.
When others question me, they cannot
know the questions and brokenness
that are in my own heart. I ask that
even in my brokenness, I would honor
you with my attitude and response.
My lack is so burdensome; I pray for
strength in my spirit. Amen.

DISCOURAGED

*This High Priest of ours understands our weaknesses, for he faced
all of the same temptations we do, yet he did not sin.
So let us come boldly to the throne of our gracious God.
There we will receive his mercy, and we will find grace to help us
when we need it most.*

—Hebrews 4:15–16

E VERY time I began to accept that I might not actually be able to give birth to a child, something would happen to me or around me to bring me back to that place of hurt. A place of discontentment, caused by my disillusioned plan for motherhood. For example, when my brother and sister-in-law announced they were expecting, I was crushed rather than overjoyed.

I remember feeling shame for the lack of joy that I knew I should be feeling for my brother, but joy was overshadowed by the pain I felt over my own inability to conceive. I wanted to be happy (and I acted as if I was at times), but inside I hurt so deeply. I can only imagine how my mother felt in that situation. She must have been overjoyed for my brother, while at the same time, her heart broke for me because she knew my desire.

It seems as though Satan knows exactly how to get us to react in an ungodly manner in situations that make us vulnerable. On the day my first niece was born, I was out of town. After receiving the call that she had arrived, I remember thinking, *now I can go home.* Arriving at the hospital a few days later, I was unexpectedly flooded with shame over my selfishness. I had caused so much hurt to others by being absent for her birth. Despite my attitude, through the grace of God, I have always adored my niece, and we share a special bond. Those sweet words, Aunt Beth, are so precious to me.

Each time I got a phone call from a friend or relative to share the news they were expecting, my heart would ache. I would long to be happy for them, but I always seemed to give in to the loss that I felt in my own life. I wanted so desperately to be able to share the same news. Again and again

I would cry. Deep inside I felt ashamed of my self-centered feelings of loss and longing. However, I didn't know how to stop. I felt as though I was being deprived of the greatest joy that a woman could ever feel. The pain I experienced every time others shared their joyful news was beyond description.

I felt so alone in my feelings, but I know now that I was not alone. And you are not alone. God knows when you are discouraged. Just when you are feeling hopeless, He will encourage your spirit. God desires to give you joy for your sadness, peace for your anger, and contentment for your longing.

Dear Lord,
Even as I long for motherhood, I
want to have genuine joy for others
when they attain what I have yet
to know. I know that joy can only
come from You. Protect my mind
from Satan's influence as I encounter
others sharing their joyful bliss. Please
remind me to lean on You, to give
You all my sorrow, and to trust You
to return peace and joy in my heart.
Amen.

DAY 11

DISAPPOINTED

Cast all your anxiety on him because he cares for you.

—1 Peter 5:7 NIV

ARE YOU disappointed in God? Disappointed in what you expected out of your Christian life and marriage? Are you faced with a God you cannot recognize for the first time in your life? What does it say about who God is and our trust in Him when we are disappointed with life?

Several years ago, a well-known contemporary Christian musician suffered the loss of one of his children. A few years later he penned a book about his family's testimony of that time. He was very transparent about his raw emotion and questions for God. He spoke about seeing a side of God he did not know, and he was unsure and unsettled about how he felt about that. About the same time, a national radio personality also lost a child to tragedy. When speaking about his family's loss, he recounted his disappointment with God.

Whether our lives are all rainbows and roses or we face disappointment and even tragic loss, God is the same. His love is the same. His peace is the same, and His care for you is the same. He never changes.

God never promised we would not encounter disappointment and loss. He understands our dismay, our questions, and our confusion. Take your disappointments to Him. Ask Him to reveal Himself to you in new ways during this time of disappointment and dissatisfaction.

Dear Lord,
All I can do is give You all my fears,
anxieties, and all my disappointments,
for I know You care for me. I love
You, Lord, despite experiencing a side
of You I do not know or understand.
Amen.

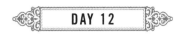

DAY 12

DEVASTATED

From the depths of despair, O LORD, I call for your help.

—PSALM 130:1

T HIS verse speaks of the heart of the barren woman. *Devastation* and *despair* are the only words that remotely describe what the realization of barrenness does to a woman's heart and mind.

The Saturday before Mother's Day a few years ago, I was signing books at a local bookstore. A precious lady sat down at the table in front of me. As she began to talk, I realized she was hurting and needed a listening ear. She began to tell me her story. Her daughter was at home having an extremely difficult time. She was hurting over the loss she was feeling because of the impossibility of having her own biological children. The daughter had knowingly married a man who was unable to have children due to cancer treatment. When they married, in that blissful cloud that most newlyweds feel, she could not imagine she would ever have any regrets. However, many years into the marriage, she was beginning to dread every Mother's Day. Her pain and feelings of loss were unbearable. As this mother began to cry, she continued her story. She wanted desperately to help her daughter to ease her pain. She had hopes that one day her daughter would adopt. Yet, her daughter said that adopting was not what she desired.

I realized this was a divine appointment! The mother's inability to cope with her daughter's hurt is what caused her to leave home that day and wander into the bookshop. I gently, lovingly, and tearfully took the mom's hand in mine and began to tell her my story. The pain of the Mother's Days that I, too, had dreaded. The hurt I knew that my own mother felt for me.

Then I had to tell this precious mother, who hurt on behalf of her own daughter, "You cannot help. As much as you want to empathize with your daughter, you cannot. You were able to have your daughter. You can hurt for her, hurt for the grandchildren you miss, but you can never know and understand the longing in the heart of a barren woman. Only God can know that pain. Only God could want more desperately for that pain to be eased and the loss lessened. It never goes away, but there is hope of joy through other opportunities to mother."

You may know this devastation. You may no longer hold hope for bearing your own children. You may believe, like this young woman, that adoption is not the same. You may dread Mother's Day. Those around you may want so desperately to help you—your mother, your husband, your friends, those with whom you counsel within your church, or even another woman who has traveled this way—but they cannot help you. Only God can, and He longs to help. Call out to Him from the depths of your despair.

Oh, God,
I know You hear my cries. I need You!
I need this pain to be soothed. I do not
understand Your ways, yet I trust in
You. Lord, please help me! Amen.

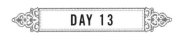

DISCONNECTED

God saved you by his grace when you believed. And you can't take credit for this; it is a gift from God. Salvation is not a reward for the good things we have done, so none of us can boast about it. For we are God's masterpiece. He has created us anew in Christ Jesus, so that we can do the good things he planned for us long ago.

—Ephesians 2:8–10

For those who have been conditioned by society and by God-given instincts to be mothers, there is a stigma attached when those expectations are not fulfilled. If you are conditioned to believe your identity and validation as a woman comes from your ability to bear children, the failure to do so can cause feelings of inadequacy that are emotionally crippling.

Not only are you well aware of feeling left out of society's expectations in general, but you also are consciously aware of being out of the loop in your own social circles. It seems everyone your age is married and having children. Their stories of night feedings, colicky babies, teething, and finding the best pediatrician leave you out of the conversation. You want so badly to join in the group, but much more than being included is a deeper desire: you want a baby of your own.

I know I felt I was a failure as a woman, a wife, and a daughter when I could not do the one thing (I told myself) God created women to do—bear children. My husband was a dad, but I wanted to join in creating a child of our own. My brother had given my parents a grandchild, but I could not. The stigma followed me even among family and friends. It was as if I was wearing a large B on my chest: *Barren.*

Too often we allow these feelings of inadequacy and failure to overshadow the knowledge that God created us all with purpose, His purpose. Paul goes further than this and says that each believer in Christ is a "masterpiece" that God has created with a plan in mind (Ephesians 2:10). Even though we may feel disconnected now, we must cling to the promise that these feelings are temporary. Though we like to place time limits on "temporary," there are none, just the assurance that it will end.

God does not want you to feel broken and disconnected. In Him you are whole and complete. Allow Him to complete His work in you for His purpose and His glory.

Dear Lord,
Bring my heart and mind in line with Your purpose for my life. I know You created me for a purpose: to glorify You. My flesh is weak. Lord, please forgive me when I give in to the stigma of barrenness and feelings of inadequacy as a woman, as Your creation, as Your daughter. Amen.

DEPRESSED

Why, my soul, are you downcast? Why so disturbed within me?
Put your hope in God, for I will yet praise him,
my Savior and my God.

—Psalm 42:11 NIV

W HY am I discouraged? Why is my heart so sad? I will put my hope in God! I will praise him again—my Savior and my God!" Psalm 42:11. This translation causes me to hear a human voice screaming from within: *What's wrong with you? Snap out of it! God is in control! Give Him praise! Put on a little more makeup and a bigger smile! Everything is fine!*

Depression is a term that describes a wide spectrum of conditions. It can range from the blahs to full-blown clinical depression that must be treated by a doctor. Sometimes depression can be resolved simply with the passage of time, but at other times it may require counseling from pastoral staff or a psychiatrist as well as medication or even hospitalization. Not all depression can be shrugged off as just the blues. Clinical depression can be caused by physical conditions that require diagnosis and treatment.

The stigma that goes with depression can be as devastating as the stigma of barrenness. We must allow ourselves to be freed of stigmas put on us by society as well as those we attach ourselves to. God has the power to free us from depression. However, just as with every other plan He has for us, He works on His timetable and in His ways. He may choose to free you supernaturally, or He may use doctors, medications, pastors, or clinics.

Elisabeth Elliot wrote in *A Chance to Die: The Life and Legacy of Amy Carmichael*, the biography of a woman who had no children but, as a missionary in India, helped many young girls escape temple prostitution, "The work of God is done on God's timetable. His answers to our prayers come always in time—His time. His thoughts are far higher than ours, His wisdom past understanding."

God is our hope and our salvation, yet we cannot put Him in a box related to infertility any more than we can in any other situation. Do not place unrealistic expectations on yourself. Be honest with yourself so you can receive the help you need. Seek guidance in the path God would have for you to take toward healing.

Dear Lord,
Why am I so sad? Why do I feel discouraged constantly? You are my hope and my healing. Lord, reveal to me how You would have me address these issues in my life. Thank You for freedom from the stigmas attached to depression. Amen.

SHANNON'S STORY

How can eyes leak this much and a heart be so broken for a love I will never know? —SHANNON WILLIAMS

I HAVE a cousin I call "Sissy." She was an only child, and I only had a brother. So we lovingly decided to be sisters from different mothers! My sissy has also been on her journey of the inability to conceive.

Just as I did, Shannon planned to be a mommy. She and her husband tried to conceive for years. As I was once told, their answer when asked about plans to have children, was, "Yes, but sometimes things don't happen the way you plan for them to." I know that feeling!

After so many years of trying unsuccessfully to have children, for medical reasons, Shannon finally had to have a hysterectomy. I know and understand her pain—the definitive void she now feels without the hope of fulfillment. I think about her husband and how he loves her so dearly. He hurts deeply for his own loss but even more for hers. I also think about her parents, who do not have the chance of being grandparents. They too are caught in the fallout of her situation. Nothing outside of God can soothe any of their pain nor ease any of their longing. However, a peace that only God can give will come in God's perfect timing.

Shannon expends some of her mother-love on her pets. She also loves children and is an amazing aunt to her nieces and nephews, as well as honorary aunt to her friends' and neighbors' children.

Not long ago, at a family gathering, we had a new tiny member join us. Shannon could not wait to hold her and blissfully held her for much of the time. Among our gathered friends and family members, Shannon and I shared a bond. I could look at her and know what she was feeling. The longing! The desires! The hurt! Yet, there was a bittersweet joy as she held that precious little baby in her arms.

Even though I know fully and understand her pain, as much as I sympathize and long to help her, I cannot. However, as we are able to share our hearts with each other and with others, we gain strength.

EMOTIONALLY AMBUSHED

Those who plant in tears will harvest with shouts of joy.
They weep as they go to plant their seed, but they sing as they
return with the harvest.

—Psalm 126:5–6

EVEN during the time I so desperately wanted to experience pregnancy and childbirth, I thought I could keep my emotions reined in pretty well. I could smile when someone told me she was pregnant, even though inside I was crying. I bought baby gifts for others in hopes of one day buying them for my own child.

At times my stoic attitude did not work, and I would be flooded with emotion. For example, I could be walking through a department store and suddenly see a display with tiny baby clothes that would send me into tears. One day, as I passed a park, I saw strollers and mothers playing with young children. I realized I had tears rolling down my cheeks. Other times, I became moody for days and could not understand why until I was reminded there was a baby shower coming up that I was expected to attend. I could go on and on.

I call them ambushes because they come out of nowhere and attack you in your most vulnerable state. Like an enemy's strategy, the purpose is to defeat you. To cause anger and jealousy. To cause you to become more impatient, to question God more, and to be swallowed up by overwhelming feelings of incompleteness and inadequacy.

God desires for you to run to Him when you encounter these ambushes. The psalmist wrote, "My heart has heard you say, 'Come and talk with me.' And my heart responds, 'LORD, I am coming'" (Psalm 27:8).

Allow Him to dry your tears, calm your fears, and remove your anger and jealousy. He desires to remind you, as His precious daughter, that He has created you for His purpose and in Him you will find complete joy.

Dear Lord,

You know my heart's cry better than I do. You are not surprised when I feel emotions rise up in me that I seem to be unable to contain. Lord, there are times that I feel defeated by the emotions that my inability to conceive have caused. Lord, please put a new song in my heart and praises of joy to You even when I encounter emotional ambushes. Amen.

HURT

He heals the brokenhearted and binds up their wounds.

—Psalm 147:3 NIV

Hurt means to feel or suffer bodily or mental pain or distress.

I N A journal from many years ago, I wrote how I felt the Lord speaking to me about the hurt in my heart caused by the reality of living with barrenness:

> Your heart is as a gaping wound. You have tried your best to hold back the bleeding with a tiny bandage. You are slowing bleeding to death as your wound continues to ooze. My desire is to heal your wound. To bind it with joy and seal it with My strength. Bring your gaping wound to Me. I will bring healing to your heart and restore to you the joy of My salvation.

This happened at a time when I thought I was beyond my limit. I found myself crying out to God in hurt and confusion. "Why do I continue to hurt so badly?" I would ask. "Why do I have no relief from the ache in my heart?" It was beyond my comprehension at the time, but I was attempting to heal my own heart with substitutes. I was merely changing the bandage when the seepage would show through, but then I would go about my business until the bandage demanded changing again. God desired to heal me by binding those wounds with the salve of the Holy Spirit.

The hurt that continues on and on in the midst of trying to conceive can be stifling. Satan wants you to stay in that place of hurt and confusion. When you are camped out there, you are not living up to the fullness that God has for you.

Jesus compared Satan to a thief who wants to destroy our lives and steal any joy we might have. "The thief does not come except to steal, and to kill, and to destroy. I have come that they may have life, and that they may have it more abundantly" (John 10:10 NKJV). But Jesus is the Good Shepherd who takes care of His sheep, protecting them and binding up their wounds. Allow Him to bind your wounds and heal your broken heart.

Dear Lord,
My pain is beyond description, yet You know it. I need Your healing for my broken heart. I need Your peace for my conflicts. I need Your joy restored to me. Thank You, Lord, for Your provision of healing for my innermost being. Amen.

ANGER

Stop being angry! Turn from your rage!
Do not lose your temper—it only leads to harm.

—Psalm 37:8

Anger: a strong feeling of displeasure and usually of antagonism.

I CAN remember being so angry when I could not conceive. It seemed like I was angry at everyone and everything. Angry that others easily achieved what I could not. Angry at those who asked if and when we might have children. Angry at my friends who were clueless as to my feelings and insecurities about wanting motherhood. Angry at my body because it would not cooperate with what I wanted.

I have to admit that I was also angry at God. Very angry. I thought that He as a loving Father God would grant all the desires of His children. But now, through wisdom gained with the years, I understand that true love, even unconditional love, places limits on what we allow our children. We do not allow them everything they want, the way they want it, and when they want it because we know it is not what is best for them. Although this often causes them to become angry, we know that one day our children will understand why we denied or delayed giving them what they so desired at the time.

Anger can cause bitterness, however it does not have to. Anger can be justified and cause growth. Yet growth can also cause pain and discomfort in itself. We are urged by Scripture not to let the sun go down on our anger (Ephesians 4:26). We are never told not to be angry. Instead we are told not to allow it to take root and bring forth bitterness and discontent. While anger comes abruptly, bitterness is more subtle. It sows slowly over time and gradually chokes the life out of our spirit.

As women of God, we must guard against anger and bitterness. We must pray our hearts only allow growth to the things of the spirit. "Think about the things of heaven, not the things of earth. For you died to this life, and your real life is hidden with Christ in God" (Colossians 3:2–3). "Since God chose you to be the holy people he loves, you must clothe yourselves with tenderhearted mercy, kindness, humility, gentleness, and patience" (v. 12).

Have you allowed anger, resentment, and even bitterness to grow out of your state of barrenness? Are you willing to offer these feelings up to God as a sacrifice, being assured He will fill your heart with joy in their place? He will. He longs to. You may not always get what you want when you want it. None of us can be assured of that. But you can be assured that He longs to see you happy, wants to give you what He knows is best for you. Offer up your heart to Him. Ask Him if there is any sin that you are unaware of in your life. As He convicts you, repent and once again find in Him your fullness of joy.

Dear Lord,
Search my heart and show me where I
have harbored anger and resentment.
Reveal to me where bitterness is taking
root. I ask that as You unveil my own
heart to me, I would be forgiven so
that I may rest in Your love for me
and seek Your joy. Amen.

GUILT

Don't let your hearts be troubled. Trust in God, and trust also in me. . . . I am leaving you with a gift; peace of mind and heart. And the peace I give is a gift the world cannot give. So don't be troubled or afraid.

—JOHN 14:1, 27

Guilt: a feeling of responsibility or remorse for some offense, crime, wrong, etc., whether real or imagined, according to dictionary.com.

G UILT is the natural human reaction when you are incapable of producing what others long for you to have. Not only did I want children born from my own womb, but so did my husband and both sets of would-be grandparents. So not only did I feel hurt, anger, and desperation, I was under the burden of guilt.

I wanted to give everyone in my family the opportunity to participate in our lives as aunts, uncles, cousins, grands, and great-grands. I wanted it all, for everyone. The feeling of guilt enabled and encouraged all the other emotions I was feeling.

I felt the most guilty when I was not genuinely happy for others who had what I desired. I missed showers, births, dinners, and other celebrations just to avoid having to act overjoyed for the mom-to-be. I knew how I felt was wrong, but it was the way I felt. And I did not know how to change my heart. I avoided any situation that would hit me with the reality of my infertility. I didn't want to be hurt any more than I already was.

The psalmists knew what it was to have such feelings, although for varying reasons. Asaph wrote in Psalm 73:21–25:

> Then I realized that my heart was bitter, and I was all torn up inside. I was so foolish and ignorant—I must have seemed like a senseless animal to you. Yet I still belong to you; you hold my right hand. You guide me with your counsel, leading me to a glorious destiny. Whom have I in heaven but you? I desire you more than anything on earth.

Guilt is a burden that weighs you down on your journey. God does not want you walking in the shadow of guilt. He longs to free you to live in the abundance He has for you. He wants you to realize that you have "a glorious destiny." Stop placing guilt trips on yourself based on how you feel or react to others. Ask God to soften your heart.

Dear Lord,
I am so weighted down by the burden
of guilt and condemnation that I
have been living under. Lord, please
free me from this guilt. Calm my fears
and fill me with Your peace as I travel
this journey. Amen.

DAY 19

BETRAYAL

My flesh and my heart may fail, but God is the strength of my heart and my portion forever.

—Psalm 73:26 NIV

Betrayal: to be unfaithful in guarding, maintaining, or fulfilling; to betray a trust; to disappoint the hopes or expectations of; or to be disloyal to, according to dictionary.com.

A S A WOMAN, created with the potential to bear children, I felt betrayed by my own body when conception was impossible. I believed that my body had revolted against what it was created with the capability to do. My questions began all over again, including the self-blaming, "Have I done something to cause this?"

Then there was the betrayal I felt when all the medications didn't work. Maybe you too have been trying unsuccessfully for years to get pregnant. All the fertility drugs you have taken have not worked. Your attempts at in vitro fertilization have let you down. You trusted your body, your doctors, and your prayers, yet you have been left unfulfilled and disappointed. Your hopes have been dashed time after time.

Has infertility caused problems in your marriage? This too seems to be part of the package. Your husband may feel betrayed by the fact that his hopes of fatherhood have also been dashed. Or maybe your feelings of hurt and betrayal come from his inability to fully understand what you are going through. He feels he has tried to understand, but his patience is wearing thin. It is possible you sometimes forget that you are both on this unwanted and unplanned journey.

As you feel let down and betrayed by the confidence you held in various fertility treatments, remember that God is your strength. He alone can carry you through this journey. Give Him your pain and betrayed feelings. Also give Him your marriage in expectation that He will heal the hurts there. He will never betray your trust in Him.

"The LORD is my strength and my shield; my heart trusts in him, and he helps me. My heart leaps for joy, and with my song I praise him" (Psalm 28:7 NIV).

Dear God,
My flesh is so weak and my heart fails
to have hope. I need Your strength. I
give You my marriage and ask that
You bring us closer together as we
travel this journey together. Amen.

GRIEF

God blesses those who mourn, for they will be comforted.

—Matthew 5:4

Grief: deep and poignant distress caused by or as if by bereavement; a cause of such suffering, according to *Merriam-Webster's Dictionary.*

EVEN when there is no death involved, as there is in a miscarriage, there is a grieving process for the barren woman. You grieve for the loss of a love you have not yet known. You grieve over the joy you feel you will never experience. You grieve for your marriage and how the dynamic is forever changed.

Grief is associated with loss, but with the barren woman it raises the question of how you can grieve over something you have not had. Motherhood is what you wanted, expected, longed for; therefore, when the inability to obtain motherhood interrupts your life as planned, grieving must take place. The overwhelming feeling of loss and dejection lead to grief.

You may be one of the thousands of women who each year experience grief because of the miscarriage of a child. Possibly you have gone through such a loss again and again. To know such sorrow is beyond comprehension, yet God longs to soothe your hurting heart.

Wherever you are on your journey—whether grief is ahead of you or behind you—God is your comfort. He knows the depths of your sorrows. He understands the loss you feel.

> He has sent me to tell those who mourn that the time of the Lord's favor has come, and with it, the day of God's anger against their enemies. To all who mourn in Israel, he will give a crown of beauty for ashes, a joyous blessing instead of mourning, festive praise instead of despair. In their righteousness, they will be like great oaks that the Lord has planted for his own glory. —Isaiah 61:2–3

Dear Lord,
My spirit grieves for a love I have not known, for a joy unfathomed and an abundant life now seemingly impossible. Lord, You hear my cries, You know every tear, and You understand my despair. I need You, Lord, to heal my spirit and to exchange my ashes of mourning for Your beauty. Amen.

DESPAIR

He lifted me out of the pit of despair,
out of the mud and the mire.
He set my feet on solid ground and steadied
me as I walked along.

—Psalm 40:2

I LOVE how Psalm 40:2 says God lifts us out of the pit, out of the mud and mire. Despair means to lose all hope; depression, hopelessness, desperation, misery, sorrow, and forlornness are all synonymous with or related words to despair *(Merriam-Webster's Dictionary)*. These terms can perfectly describe the feelings brought on by the reality of barrenness.

In the midst of despair, you feel as though you have been sent headlong into a dark, bottomless pit. No matter how you try to climb out, you find yourself more and more immobile in the mud and mire of gloom and anguish.

You must know that you cannot pull yourself out of the pit. All the smiles, seemingly happy attitudes, or times you tell yourself (or others tell you) to "snap out of it" will not lessen the despair. However, you must remember, you are not hopeless. Christ is your hope and your Redeemer. When you find yourself wallowing in the mire, look up and cry out for your hope to rescue you.

The psalmist reminds us that there is no reason to give up hope: "He set my feet on solid ground and steadied me as I walked along." Despair is temporal, if we allow ourselves to be rescued. We will no longer be held down by our feelings but free to continue growing in faith. What hope!

Allow Christ to rescue you today. Allow Him to free you from the bonds that hold you back from all He has for you. Stop trying to handle this alone. This is bigger than you comprehend. He wants to bring you through this and use your testimony for His glory.

Dear God,
Help! I cannot do this on my own. I
feel as though I have been swallowed
up in darkness. I need You now. I
long to be free from this pit dug by
my own emotions. My hope is in You,
Lord. Amen.

MY STORY

We can make our plans, but the LORD determines our steps.

—PROVERBS 16:9

I HAD problems with my reproductive system all through my teens and into adulthood, and those problems just increased with age and time. However, when I continued to have difficulty getting pregnant, I assumed it was a matter of timing and that eventually I would conceive.

When I married at age 23, my husband had sole custody of his two precious sons, ages two and three. So I was enjoying motherhood but longed to have a child of my own. The boys were still young when I began having severe menstrual problems. When I was 25, my Pap smear came back showing signs of precancerous cells. The decision had to be made to have a hysterectomy. To say I was devastated would be an understatement.

I was on a pathway in life that I never expected to travel. Suddenly, I was the barren woman described in Scripture. How would I ever be "a happy mother of children" (Psalm 113:9 NIV)? Moreover, how would I ever find contentment? Yet I clung to what I claimed as God's promise that I would be a happy mother of children. I was unsettled about what seemed to be God's plan for my life. For years, I continued to believe for a miracle and the blessing of a baby, all the while I was missing out on the ones God had already placed in my life—"my" two precious little boys.

Something inside me was convinced that I was less of a mother because I had not actually given birth to them. I felt the need for validation as a woman, a wife, and a mother. Looking back, that deeply saddens me. I had been blessed with the awesome gift and the enormous responsibility of being a mother to two boys who needed me. And, oh, how desperately, I needed them. God had chosen me to be the mother to those boys and for them to be my children. God brought us together to bring Him glory. They did not need just any mother; they needed the mother God had created for them, the mother whose godly heritage had been passed on through generations of mothers before her. I was that chosen mother.

All through the years, I told my precious boys they couldn't be any more mine if I had given birth to them. It is beyond comprehension how I loved them as my own yet still longed for more. I also remember listening to others talk about their inability to conceive and how they finally had to answer the question for themselves, "Do we want to be pregnant, or do we want to be parents?" I wanted both! Yet, I was already a mother. I was missing the miracle that I was living while I was praying for the one I wanted.

When I allowed God to reveal His plan for my life instead of begging Him to go along with my plans, He gave me more children than I imagined, while also opening the door to the world. When my sons were young, we opened our home to host international students. The students would come to stay with us and become a part of our family for nine months while they attended a local school. This was a chance for us to minister to them as we shared the love of Christ with them. I am blessed to consider myself a second (American) mom to one French young man (not yet married), one German young woman who is now married and has my first little German "granddaughter." I am also honorary American mom to another young woman in Uruguay who is married and has another of my "grands by grace!"

Today at 48, I am mom by grace to my two handsome boys, and to my beautiful and sweet daughter-in-law! In 2002, I was remarried after a devastating divorce. My sons were teens when I remarried and became mother (by marriage) to two lovely daughters and one more handsome son. I have six of the most beautiful and wonderful grandchildren in the world—two boys and four girls—and one precious baby boy already in heaven. Now, that is God!

I thought my prayers and my plans were delayed. My life, God's plan for my life, has been destined from before the foundation of the world. His plans were for my good and to bring Him glory! "'For I know the plans I have for you,' declares the LORD, 'plans to prosper you and not to harm you, plans to give you hope and a future'" (Jeremiah 29:11 NIV). Words cannot express the joy in my life! God has blessed me beyond measure!

I don't know how God is working in your life. He may give you many children, or those desires may remain unfulfilled dreams. He may fill your life with a community of friends and act in ways you would not expect. But, I want to encourage you—however God chooses to work, He can bring beauty out of ashes. He's done it in my life, and I know that He can do it in yours.

A HAPPY WOMAN

*He settles the childless woman in her home as a
happy mother of children.*

—Psalm 113:9 NIV

I HAVE come to look at this verse with deep appreciation and, I believe, much more wisdom and understanding than in the past. I am now truly settled and recognize that I am a blessed mother of children. Being settled came only from the same gracious Source who provided the blessing, the Father I so often questioned before. Now I thank Him for not answering my prayers my way, and I even thank Him for allowing me to hurt and to grow as I unknowingly complied with His will for my life rather than my own.

One thing I have learned is that a genetic bond is not a necessary part of being a mother. I could always see how blessed women were who experienced the gift of motherhood naturally and easily. But now, through grace, I recognize the honor bestowed on all who are called "mother" or are looked on as a type of mother in any way.

Possibly, motherhood has come differently to you. You may have younger siblings or nieces and nephews whose lives you invest in and with whom you share a special bond. Maybe you are a teacher and have an almost maternal affection for and relationship with some of your students. Maybe you mentor young girls or counsel troubled teens in your community. Or, if you don't, maybe you should. There are many opportunities that the Lord opens to us—ways that we can fill needs in the lives of children and fill voids in our own.

Oh, what a mighty God we serve. What a loving Heavenly Father to give us the opportunities that our bodies did not afford us. To bless us with the love of children. To gift us with the heart of a mother, the strength of a mother, and the joy of a mother. How blessed we are!

You may be at a point in your journey that you find no hope in today's Scripture because you look at it in only the most literal way. It may be beyond your understanding how you could become a happy woman while still being childless. You may not comprehend how you can be settled or ever be content with barrenness. The questions of why, how, and when are all futile. However, God is able to make a way when there seems to be no way for "with God nothing will be impossible" (Luke 1:37 NKJV).

Dear Lord,
I long to be happy. I long to be settled.
I am confused as to how I can be
barren and happy. Yet, I know Your
love for me and I trust in Your word.
Lord, I want to be the "mother" You
created me to be. Amen.

GRACE TO SUSTAIN

But he said to me, "My grace is sufficient for you, for my power is made perfect in weakness." Therefore I will boast all the more gladly about my weaknesses, so that Christ's power may rest on me.

—2 Corinthians 12:9 NIV

SOMETIMES the phrase, "God's grace is sufficient" is thrown around almost flippantly in Christian circles. It seems to be the answer for anything people have not encountered themselves and do not really understand. This may be especially true of the struggles you are going through on this unwanted journey of infertility. For most women, motherhood comes easily and naturally. Therefore they have no point of reference when dealing with childless women. They do not mean to be hurtful in their comments, but many times their comments have that result.

When Christ said to Paul that His grace was sufficient—actually, more than enough—there was no mistake in His wording. God's word is infallible. Yet, as a young woman going through my own journey of the inability to conceive, I cringed when someone smiled and threw that Scripture at me. I knew it was true, but that did not lessen how distraught I felt at the time. I did feel weak. I was weak. And I was not concerned about my spirit being strong; I wanted my body to produce babies. I know this all may sound harsh, but God knew my feelings then and He knows my repentant heart now.

Now only by the all-sufficient grace of God can I boast about how He changed my heart, strengthened my spirit, and fills me daily with His power to share my testimony.

You may be where I was when others spoke those words to me. Or you may understand more fully and rely on God's grace to see you through. You may be farther down the pathway in your journey, and you may fully know of His power to sustain and to allow you to share with others. Wherever you are, God's grace is the same. All-sufficient. More than enough.

Dear God,
Thank You for Your all-sustaining grace. The grace that only allows me to see where I am and not where I have been or where I am going. Your grace soothes the ache and brings me hope. I rely on Your grace for strength as I desire to bring honor to You and testify of Your grace and mercy. Amen.

DAY 24

GOD'S PLAN IS PERFECT

Now all glory to God, who is able, through his mighty power at work within us, to accomplish infinitely more than we might ask or think.

—Ephesians 3:20

During those years of praying for children, God revealed other Scriptures to me. Isaiah 54:2–3 states,

> Enlarge your house; build an addition. Spread out your home, and spare no expense! For you will soon be bursting at the seams.

WHENEVER I came to such Scriptures, I would express praise and thanksgiving, believing they were for me. I never sought God's will or yielded myself to how His plan would be brought about. I never abandoned my own plans long enough for Him to show me that His plan was already in motion. I just continued to plan for the way I expected it to be.

With my plan, I would have experienced 40 weeks of pregnancy, the discomfort of labor, and the joys of motherhood. But my motherhood could have been short-lived because of cystic fibrosis and how pregnancy would have ravaged my body. God's plan made provision for me to be healthy, live a long and prosperous life, and yet be a blessed mother of children. His plan brought honor and glory to Him. By the loving grace of God, I am also now enraptured in the immeasurable joy that I find in the blissful state of "Nanahood."

For so long, I thought my prayers were being ignored, and I could not understand why my plans were not coming to fruition. Yet, the plans that God had for my life were perfect. His plans have been destined for me from before the foundation of the world. His plans were for my good and to bring Him glory.

"For I know the plans I have for you," declares the LORD, "plans to prosper you and not to harm you, plans to give you hope and a future." —Jeremiah 29:11 NIV

Do you trust that God has a perfect plan for your life? Are you thankful for His perfect plan, which promises to far exceed your imagination or expectation? Give Him praise, even before you fully comprehend how His plan will take place. Remember, His plan is perfect.

Dear Lord,
I believe that Your plan is perfect for
my life. Please forgive me when I do
not like the path I am on. I thank
You and praise You for far exceeding
my imagination and expectations for
my life. Lord, I love You and I trust
you. Amen.

DAY 25

THE GREATER PICTURE

*And we know that God causes everything to work together
for the good of those who love God and are called according to his
purpose for them.*

—Romans 8:28

OUR desires paint a minute picture for us to focus on. However, God's plan is far beyond our scope of vision. When the children of Israel left Egypt and set out for the Promised Land, they knew where they had come from, and they knew the promise of deliverance. Yet, the middle of the picture was missing: the details. I often wonder if many of them would have stayed behind in Egypt instead of going on the journey if they had known what lay in store for them (40 years of wandering in the wilderness!).

We are no different than the Israelites. We want to know where we are going, what to expect along the way, and how quickly we can get there. We do not like speed bumps, detours, or road blocks. We want to take shortcuts and just hit the highlights.

God's desire is to take every detail along our journey and create an extravagant tapestry to honor and bring glory to Him. He does not take shortcuts for He knows the interruptions along the way create the depth and hues of color.

Oh, what an amazingly beautiful tapestry God has created in and with my life. I praise Him for the love and joy He has brought into my heart and my life. His picture, the greatest picture, is beyond imagination and brilliant in the color of abundance.

God wove the priceless fabric that is your life. He stitched every thread of the vibrant colors into place to create His masterpiece for His eternal glory. Don't pull against the Master as He perfects His work in you. You will be amazed by the beauty beyond description.

Dear Lord,
I grow anxious and weary. I long to see Your finished work, when You have only begun. I long for the beauty when I cannot fathom it. I long for light and life when I feel submerged in darkness. Lord, thank You for Your promise to bring everything into focus and make it honoring to You. Amen.

DAY 26

BLESSINGS IN DISGUISE

*"For my thoughts are not your thoughts, neither are your ways
my ways," declares the* Lord. *"As the heavens are higher than the
earth, so are my ways higher than your ways and my thoughts
than your thoughts."*

—Isaiah 55:8–9 NIV

L ATE one night we received a call from our oldest daughter, who lived in another part of the state, two hours south of us. She had just given birth to our second grandson. The call that should have been blissful quickly turned prayerful. Our grandson was being airlifted to Birmingham. Due to our daughter's incapacity, she was not able to come with him, which sent us rushing to the hospital. When we arrived, nothing could have prepared me for what I encountered. In an open bed, with life-sustaining tubes, wires, and monitors connected to much of his tiny body, was our newest precious grandson. He had been born with three different types of heart defects. I remember crying silent tears. I looked into his face, longing to hold his hand that was outstretched with an IV in it. The pain was so deep that no noise came out. But, as I stood at his bedside and stroked his head, I also remember how desperately I wanted the same thing for this grandson I had wanted for every other grandchild. I wanted to hold him, hug him, sing to him. I wanted to hear his cry, see his smile, hear his laughter, and watch him play. I wanted him to know how much he was loved.

Due to unforeseeable circumstances, my husband and I became the proxy for our daughter, allowing us to be there for our grandson because she could not. This allowed me to be able to have the gracious gift of firsts with our newest grandchild. Outside of the medical teams, I was blessed to be the first one in our family to hold him. I will never forget that first time, tears rolled down my cheeks as I gave God praise for this little life.

Not knowing how long we would have him or what we might encounter throughout his life, I did know that every life has purpose and God destined that child for His purpose.

I also was allowed many more blessings of firsts: the first in our family to feed him, the first one to change his diaper, the first to bathe him. I experienced firsts like I'd never had the opportunity with the others. What a blessing! Such a gift of grace by my Father in heaven who knew my heart. He knew my heart because He had placed it within me.

Because of all the joy that God had placed in my life through my children and then grandchildren, my heart was blissfully content. I no longer sought after the things I once thought I could not live without. When I settled in the plans the Lord had for me, He gave me the desires of my heart. He had not forgotten me.

Maybe you are missing blessings in disguise because you are expecting them your way. Maybe you have misappropriated God's gifts of grace as you long for more. Possibly you feel as though you will never find peace or contentment without the one thing you have not been successful in attaining. Let God speak to you. He has not forgotten you.

Dear Lord,
Thank You for all the blessings in my life. Help me to recognize Your blessings, even when they come in unexpected ways. Amen.

GIFTS OF GRACE

Every good and perfect gift is from above, coming down from the Father of the heavenly lights, who does not change like shifting shadows.

—JAMES 1:17 NIV

I OFTEN refer to my children and grandchildren as my gifts of grace. God put the desire in my heart to be a mother, but He chose how to fulfill it. Through His plan I have lived a long and abundant life, full of joy—and children.

I never planned to marry and divorce—no one does—but it happened to me. Through my first marriage, I was blessed to raise two amazing boys and bring them up in the nurture and admonition of the Lord. Because they were ages two and three when I assumed the role as mommy, that's all they ever knew. What a distinct honor in knowing I was chosen by God to be their mother. When I remarried, I became a mom in different ways. My husband had custody of his three children, but they had an ongoing relationship with their mom, so I took on more of a mentor role to the girls, and a part-time mom to the son. I never used the terms *stepson* or *stepdaughter*. They, through marriage and by grace, are my children also. I am so blessed to share them with their mom.

When our first grandson was born, I was gifted by grace once again to take part in something I never thought possible. I became Nana. What bliss indeed! I since have been blessed with six more grandchildren. Six more gifts of grace!

I have the wonderful opportunity to enjoy common bonds with each of the loving gifts God has blessed me with in my children and grandchildren. Yet each relationship is as uniquely special and as completely different as they are.

What an amazing blessing and gift of grace from a loving Father who knew all along the joy that awaited me! With every tear that He caught and placed in His bottle years before, He knew one day new tears would flow from the joyful heart of this mother and nana.

I will bless my people and their homes around my holy hill. And in the proper season I will send the showers they need. There will be showers of blessing.

—Ezekiel 34:26

Dear God,
Thank You for Your gifts of grace.
Thank You for Your showers of
blessing that refresh me just when
I need them. You are my God, and
I will forever sing Your praises.
Amen.

DAY 28

BE SETTLED

Be still, and know that I am God; I will be exalted among the nations, I will be exalted in the earth.

—Psalm 46:10 NIV

THE last thing I wanted while on my journey through barrenness was to be settled. I was not obedient in being still or in listening to God to know He was my peace. My place of rest. I just continued on my way, in my way, unsettled, unrested, and uneasy in every step I took and every direction I turned.

I think of a child, when they are in want and disquieted. We draw them close, speak gently to them in attempts to quiet them, to settle them. We lovingly urge them to be still and listen to our instruction. Only in their stillness and quietness can and will they be comforted, settled.

David put his desire to feel settled this way in Psalm 131:1–2 (NIV):

> My heart is not proud, LORD, my eyes are not haughty; I do not concern myself with great matters or things too wonderful for me. But I have calmed and quieted myself, I am like a weaned child with its mother; like a weaned child I am content.

Things may not be as you hoped for your life. You are the disquieted child who is in need. As a loving Father, God wants to settle you in the place He has for you. Your place of abundance. Your place of rest. Your place of joy. When you are settled in His plan for your life, He will be exalted.

Lord,
Teach me to be still and to listen to
Your voice. I want to know Your heart
for me. I know You are God; Lord,
help me to know and comprehend
that You are my *God. Settle me in*
the life You have for me. Amen.

CONTENTMENT IN CHRIST

I am not saying this because I am in need, for I have learned to be content whatever the circumstances. I know what it is to be in need, and I know what it is to have plenty. I have learned the secret of being content in any and every situation, whether well fed or hungry, whether living in plenty or in want.

—Philippians 4:11–12 NIV

THE Apostle Paul learned the secret of contentment and was able to say in Philippians 4:11, "for I have learned to be content whatever the circumstances." Although he was writing more about physical needs, such as hunger, what he learned applies to all our needs—even our emotional needs, which at times feel so physical. He learned the secret of contentment by drawing closer to Christ despite outward circumstances that were painful or stressful.

Our loving Heavenly Father has placed the "heart of a mother" in women, whether you birth, adopt, foster, minister to, or teach children. Whether they are your own children, stepchildren, orphans, nieces, nephews, or neighbors. Whatever your opportunity is, take it to become the "mother" God created you to be, all the while praying that His grace will create a heart of contentment within you.

Your fullness of joy, your life, and your salvation are found in Christ. There is no other place you can be complete and content. When you find yourself wandering in the darkness, feeling alone and longing for more, cling tightly to Him. His grace will light your way and bring you comfort. In your lack of understanding the plans of God, you may become restless and impatient as you travel your unique journey, but God is with you.

Cry out to Him as the psalmist did in Psalm 63:1–8 (NIV):

You, God, are my god, earnestly I seek you; I thirst for you, my body longs for you, in a dry and parched land where there is no water. I have seen you in the sanctuary and beheld your power and your glory. Because your love is better than life, my lips will glorify you. I will praise you as long as I live, and in your name I will lift up my hands. I will be fully satisfied as with the richest of foods; with singing lips my mouth will praise you. On my bed I remember you; I think of you through the watches of the night. Because you are my help, I sing in the shadow of your wings. I cling to you; your right hand upholds me.

Dear Lord,
I long for contentment. I am so restless and feel lacking because I have not born children of my own. I know You can and will bring me to that place of peace within. I cling desperately to the hope that is in You. Amen.

BEAUTY OUT OF BARRENNESS

You have turned my mourning into joyful dancing. You have taken away my clothes of mourning and clothed me with joy, that I might sing praises to you and not be silent. O LORD my God, I will give you thanks forever!

—PSALM 30:11–12

I AM thankful that I am now honestly overjoyed when those I care for proclaim that they are expecting. I am overjoyed because I know that the journey they are embarking on is full of joy beyond comprehension.

When I finally allowed Him, God changed my heart and my attitude. Then, fully in line with His character, He gave me a lifetime of something spectacular.

The beauty that my life has beheld because of my loving Heavenly Father! The love that He has poured into my heart! The joy He has filled my life with is not only unspeakable but also immeasurable! The matchless love I have experienced through little hands and big hearts has far outweighed the sadness I experienced through barrenness. Truly, my Lord has brought beauty out of my barrenness.

Give Father God your mourning and He will give you a song for dancing. Dispose of your mourning garments and allow him to clothe you with His joy. Sing His praises, shout with joy. Never cease to praise Him for He is Jehovah Rapha, the Lord who heals.

> We wait in hope for the LORD; he is our help and our shield. In him our hearts rejoice, for we trust in his holy name. May your unfailing love be with us, LORD, even as we put our hope in you. —Psalm 33:20–22 NIV

Dear Father God,

I pray for my sister today. You know her heart, her hurt. You alone know the depths of her despair and the tears she sheds for a love not yet known. For a desire and a longing that seems stronger than life itself at times. As her weeping endures for the night, let joy come in the morning. I pray You will turn her mourning into dancing and clothe her with joy unspeakable and full of glory. May her life and testimony bring honor and glory to You. Amen.

"*Today is mine. Tomorrow is none of my business. If I peer anxiously into the fog of the future, I will strain my spiritual eyes so that I will not see clearly what is required of me now.*"

ELISABETH ELLIOT

Understanding brings healing...

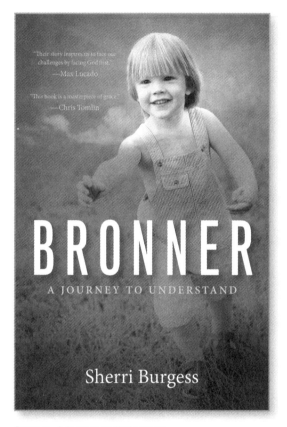

Bronner: A Journey to Understand

Sherri Burgess

ISBN-13: 978-1-62591-500-9

N164109 · $16.99

God teaches and refines us through pain and suffering. Author Sherri Burgess, wife of Rick Burgess of *The Rick and Bubba Show*, knows this to be true. After the earthly death of her youngest son, Bronner, Burgess asked, "Why?" And God answered.

Journey with her through this powerful testimony of healing to understand the purpose behind the pain. An empowering resource for book-club discussion or small-group Bible study, this is much more than simply a retelling of an inspiring story. It is a call to action beckoning us to know our Holy God like never before.

GIVE A GIFT OF HOPE!

30 Days of Hope for Peaceful Living

Mark Bethea

ISBN-13: 978-1-59669-437-8
N154115 · $9.99

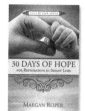

30 Days of Hope for Restoration in Infant Loss

Maegan Roper

ISBN-13: 978-1-59669-438-5
N154116 · $9.99

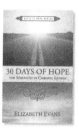

30 Days of Hope for Strength in Chronic Illness

Elizabeth Evans

ISBN-13: 978-1-59669-465-1
N164105 · $9.99

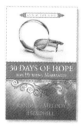

30 Days of Hope for Joy through a Child's Severe Illness

Gale Alexander

ISBN-13: 978-1-59669-475-0
N164115 · $9.99

30 Days of Hope for Comfort in Infertility

Elizabeth Evans

ISBN-13: 978-1-59669-464-4
N164104 · $9.99

30 Days of Hope for Hurting Marriages

Randy and Melody Hemphill

ISBN-13: 978-1-62591-507-8
N174106 · $9.99

For information, visit NewHopePublishers.com.

New Hope® Publishers is a division of WMU®, an international organization that challenges Christian believers to understand and be radically involved in God's mission. For more information about WMU, go to wmu.com. More information about New Hope books may be found at NewHopePublishers.com. New Hope books may be purchased at your local bookstore.

Please go to
NewHopePublishers.com
for more helpful information about
30 Days of Hope for Comfort in Infertility.

If you've been blessed by this book,
we would like to hear your story.
The publisher and author welcome your comments and
suggestions at: newhopereader@wmu.org.